CHOOSING & U

House Beautiful

CHOOSING & USING

Lighting

Joanna Copestick

Ebury Press
London

First published 1995

1 3 5 7 9 10 8 6 4 2

This edition published in 1995 by
Ebury Press
Random House, 20 Vauxhall Bridge
Road, London SW1V 2SA

Random House Australia (Pty)
Limited
20 Alfred Street, Milsons Point,
Sydney, New South Wales 2061,
Australia

Random House New Zealand Limited
18 Poland Road, Glenfield,
Auckland 10, New Zealand

Random House South Africa (Pty)
Limited
PO Box 337, Bergvlei, South Africa

Random House UK Limited
Reg. No. 954009

A CIP catalogue record for this book
is available from the British Library.

ISBN 009 179036 0

Editor: Emma Callery
Designed by Jerry Goldie Graphic
Design, London

Colour separations by HBM Print Ltd
Printed and bound in Singapore by
Tien Wah Press

CONTENTS

INTRODUCTION

Welcome to our *Choosing and Using* series of practical books. Every home-owner knows the problems that so often go with the pride in creating a comfortable and attractive place to live. So with this in mind, our clear guides have been created to form a useful and inspirational series to keep on hand while you choose and use the essential elements for every room. Lighting, for example, is made quite simple with this book. Once you know about the different types of lighting - whether they be for background, accent, task or information lighting - you can position your lamps around the house for the best effect.

The other books in the series cover aspects in an equally detailed way and I know you'll find each book as useful and inspiring as every issue of *House Beautiful* magazine.

Pat Roberts Cairns

Pat Roberts Cairns
Editor

Left *Candlelight is soft and subtle, and is the perfect way to add an atmospheric glow to any room.*

CHOOSING LIGHTING

Good lighting can transform a room from a dingy 'box' into an intimate, atmospheric living space, by the simple flick of a switch. Yet more often than not, rooms are lit by a single pendant light suspended from the ceiling, with no supplementary lighting. This is the worst possible solution, since an overhead pendant fitted with a tungsten filament light bulb casts an indiscriminate glare that fiercely illuminates all corners of the room. The result is a bland, non-directional spread of light that creates no atmosphere whatsoever and can subdue the architectural strengths of a room.

Two centuries ago, people may have lacked our modern technology, but their rooms, lit by the flickering flames of fires, candles and gas lamps, were full of warmth and intimacy. This was because they lit only specific areas where they were eating, talking or reading – rather than entire rooms – and created inviting pools of light that offered visual variety. It is this welcoming, intimate atmosphere that should be the aim of any successful modern lighting system.

Lighting can make or break your decorative scheme. It highlights or disguises a room's features, defines its colours and contours, enhances its size and generally helps to create a background mood, so it helps to know how to make it work for you.

Right *Successful lighting can be anything from a simple Japanese paper lantern to a high-tech halogen light source. The art is to look carefully at a room and consider its uses before committing yourself to a specific light.*

PLANNING THE LIGHT

Before considering which artificial lighting sources are the most suitable for your purposes, it is important to assess the effect of natural daylight on your living space.

It has been proven that people are more cheerful on bright, sunny days. Those who suffer from depression and live in dark houses have been known to improve their mood considerably simply by installing additional lighting in their homes.

CHOOSING DECOR

Your choice of decoration should be guided by the amount of natural light each room receives. In a north-facing living room, for example, be careful not to use dark wall or floor coverings. If you use pale neutral colours such as yellow, rust or pink on ceiling and floor, the natural light will reflect off these surfaces. This really helps to cheer up dark rooms on dull-weather days.

In rooms with south-facing windows where you will get lots of sunlight, the room may become too hot in the summer. You can counteract this by using a colder colour such as blue, emerald or aqua in your decorative scheme.

MEASURING NATURAL DAYLIGHT

❖ Work out in which direction your house and more specifically, your living room, faces and calculate how much of the day will bring you bright, natural light.
❖ Tailor your plans accordingly, by making sure that you provide supplementary lighting for dark corners. In this way, overcast days can be enlivened by a subtle application of artificial lighting.

Left The natural light in this room has been harnessed and used well. Open shutters allow light to filter into a pale-coloured room.

LIGHT AND SHADOW

The difference between walking down a tree-lined avenue with sunlight dancing through the branches and strolling underneath the dull sameness of a cloud-soaked sky can be explained by shadow. The contrast between light and shade casts pleasing variations on surfaces and textures to which we all respond positively. Without shadow, texture cannot be revealed and the overall feel of a room becomes two-dimensional and uninteresting.

Modern lighting technology has moved on from the early days of bland, harsh light and now consists of a more sophisticated palette which you can use to 'paint' a room. Halogen light, for example, matches more exactly the white, clear tone of natural light and has revolutionized domestic lighting during the last two decades.

A mixture of light and shadow is important in creating atmosphere, so vary the position of your lights. Bright, evenly-lit rooms quickly become monotonous and stressful, so why not consider creating pin-

Above This charming loft room with scumbled plaster-pink walls needs only a small bedside table lamp to throw subtle shadows across the room. A simple but highly effective lighting solution.

Right Often a small pool of light in the corner of a room will provide both accent and mood lighting at the same time.

To help you create effective lighting arrangements, here are some ideas to think about:

❖ Assess the level of natural daylight.

❖ Consider which type of lighting will give you your desired amount of light (see pages 16-21).

❖ If planning lighting from scratch (see pages 14-15), decide whether you want to consult a lighting designer who can organize the planning, design and installation of an integrated lighting system.

❖ Choose light fittings (see pages 22-5) which blend in with the room's decorative style.

❖ Carry out any wiring work before you start to decorate or install new floor coverings.

❖ Use colour in your decorative scheme to enhance the available light.

❖ Use dimmers (see page 31). Dimming switches are an easy way to create variable moods within a space to suit changing needs at different times.

❖ Think practically. Remember that unfixed fittings such as table lamps and standard lamps can easily be knocked over by small children, if left in inappropriate places. So they are best used in tandem with fixed lighting to give you a greater flexibility .

points of light in different areas of the room at different heights by using a combination of uplighters, table lamps and wall-fixed lights?

THE RIGHT ANGLE

❖ Shadows are produced only when light is directional, so experimenting to get the angle right is crucial.
❖ If you graze light across the brickwork above an open fireplace from an angle, you will highlight its inherent rough texture.
❖ If you light it straight on with a flat, even light it will just look dull.

STARTING FROM SCRATCH

If you are planning to completely redecorate a room, this is the time to properly plan your lighting requirements. Chasing wires through plaster for wall-mounted lights is a messy, costly job that should only be carried out if you are renovating from scratch. Think about your lighting at the same time as you are deciding what colour to paint or paper the walls and what style of furnishings you favour.

The ideal way to wire a room is by installing two or three lighting circuits to control wall (accent), ceiling (background) and table (task) lamps and programme them into dimmable wall switches. However, most people do not have the financial resources to embark on such expensive rewiring procedures. Luckily there are ways of altering a lighting system without resorting to lifted floorboards and disturbed plasterwork.

The mere addition of a number of dimmer switches, coupled with some floor standing uplighters, can have the same overall effect as specially installed wall lights. The added advantage is that they are movable and adjustable. Likewise, carefully chosen floor and table lamps can transform the atmosphere of a room as completely as can costly, sophisticated lighting circuits.

HOW WILL THE ROOM BE USED?

When planning the lighting, consider the main uses to which your room will be put. Examine the different types of lighting on pages 16–21 and select the right elements to gather in one room.

Kitchens and bathrooms, for instance, require very different treatment from living and dining rooms. In a living room, you are likely to need a background dimmable light, wall lights, accent lighting and task or desk lamps for reading, watching TV or sewing by. Additionally, you may need some specific decorative lighting to highlight pictures or displays of treasured objects. Or in a dining room you may decide to install a chandelier with a dimmer switch (see page 42) for eating by, or for playtime if your room doubles up as a playroom. Whatever your requirements, work out the kind of effect you want and then list what fittings you will need.

LIGHTING FOR SAFETY

❖ Don't forget that safe lighting is important, especially if the very old or very young live with you.

❖ Bad lighting can lead to serious accidents, while trailing wires present a dangerous hazard.

❖ Adequate lighting is particularly important in kitchens, bathrooms and workshops, as well as on stairs and landings.

There are three main design areas to consider when choosing new lighting:

❖ The light source - the quality and quantity of the light emitted by the bulb.

❖ The light fitting - how it looks, directs and distributes light.

❖ How you will eventually want to position the light fittings within the room.

Above *This small bathroom benefits from carefully placed wall lights which illuminate both the room and the mirror above the sink without creating too much glare.*

TYPES OF LIGHTING

There are several types of lighting which make up a balanced scheme. Lighting has many functions, and can be used alone or in combination, depending on your room and the tasks you plan to carry out there.

BACKGROUND LIGHTING

Background lighting is a general light consisting of an overall background sweep of light. It is usually provided by a fixed central overhead fitting to ensure a level of general visibility in a room. Simple and cheap, overhead fittings form the basis of most domestic lighting systems, but they can create unpleasant shadows or cast too much yellow light when fitted with ordinary tungsten filament bulbs. Used alone, these bulbs do not provide enough atmospheric light for a comfortable living room.

This form of lighting can sometimes be dispensed with completely in a living room. Instead, central overhead fittings can be replaced by recessed low-voltage halogen ceiling lights, complemented by floor-standing uplighters, wall lights or table lamps. Pendants are useful though for bedrooms and workrooms, and for lighting eating areas in the dining room. They always provide a strong background light.

All background lighting should be dimmable so you can vary mood. Don't forget that you can also alter the type of background light produced by using different kinds of lampshades.

Downlights recessed into a ceiling give a discreet light. Because the beams shine straight down and the bulbs are hidden, they do not cause any glare but produce soft pools of atmospheric light. They are expensive to install though, and may have to be concealed in a false ceiling.

BACKGROUND LIGHT SOURCES

❖ Single overhead, central pendant (to provide general lighting for a room)

❖ Opaque uplighters (to light a ceiling)

❖ Wall-washers (to throw light across a wall and act as a reflector)

❖ Fluorescent strip lights concealed behind coving or architraves (to provide general atmosphere).

Where to use background lighting

❖ Living rooms

❖ Kitchens

❖ Workrooms

❖ Work spaces.

Left *Uplighters cast dramatic beams of light in a simply decorated room. They emphasize the architectural features and draw the eye upwards towards them.*

ACCENT LIGHTING

This puts a specific focus on a single object or detail in à room. It can act as a decorative device or as a highlighter, emphasizing the colours of a favourite painting or display of objects, picking out a focal point, or simply providing dramatic washes of light on a coloured wall. In emphasizing the positive elements of a room, ugly features are disguised by being left in darkness. Whereas background lighting provides a flat layer of light, accent lighting reinstates character and interest into a scheme. Glassware in particular looks most effective when accent-lit from behind, because of its translucence. Spotlights, wall lights and downlights can all play an effective part in accent lighting and specialist lighting shops will advise on their use.

ACCENT LIGHTING SOURCES

❖ Low-voltage halogen spotlights

❖ Floodlights or mini-spots

❖ Low-voltage halogen table lamps

❖ Picture lights (tungsten strips or low-voltage halogen).

Where to use accent lighting

❖ Living rooms

❖ Dining rooms

❖ Rooms with strong architectural features to focus on.

Left Two table lamps placed either side of a feature fireplace provide accent light as well as visual relief in this long, high-ceilinged living room.

Right This reproduction spotlight gives off a jewel-like glow which highlights a collection of old family photographs.

TASK LIGHTING

For reading, working or cooking, task lighting is a localized light source for specific activities where a concentrated beam of light is needed. Such lighting is ideal, for example, on a desk in a study, or as recessed strip lighting fitted below kitchen units to light a work surface. Localized and multi-directional forms of lighting should be positioned carefully so that they do not create shadows on your work.

Since task lights are self-illuminating, they provide an ideal background light source for watching television or working at a VDU. Place them above or to one side of the screen.

INFORMATION LIGHTING

Designed for safety and comfort, this type of lighting highlights areas such as stairways, key holes or garage doors, where it is not the quality of the light itself, but what it is illuminating, that is important. Information lighting is also known as utility lighting.

TASK LIGHTING SOURCES

❖ Desk lamps

❖ Clip-on spots

❖ Anglepoise lamps

❖ Adjustable, directional table lamps (fit them with crown-silvered, non-glare bulbs to diffuse the light and nearly opaque lampshades to stop further glare)

❖ Compact fluorescent strips

❖ Low-voltage tungsten-halogen lamps.

Where to use task lighting

❖ Kitchens

❖ Bathrooms

❖ Studies

❖ Living rooms

❖ Bedrooms.

INFORMATION LIGHTING SOURCES

❖ Spotlights

❖ Weatherproof high intensity discharge (HID) lamps

❖ Angled uplighters.

Where to use information lighting

❖ Halls and stairways

❖ Landings

❖ Entrances

❖ Around garage doors

❖ In gardens.

Above left *A fabulous modern kitchen is made even more special by the addition of energy-saving light bulbs attached to simple metal fittings. They highlight work areas while providing mood lighting for the rest of the room.*

Left *Task lights are absolutely essential for work areas, to emphasize your work and to help prevent eye strain.*

LIGHT FITTINGS

Your choice of light fittings will depend to a large extent on your style of furnishings and personal taste. If you prefer traditional-looking pendant lights, then make sure that you install matching or sympathetic wall and table lights which will echo your decorative theme.

The new generation of low-voltage halogen table lamps and uplighters do tend to be of a modern design, but there is no reason why they cannot be subtly integrated into an older house. There are now so many different light designs available that if you search around you will find something which suits you and your room.

WHAT'S WHAT

Above Pendant lights don't have to look predictable. This glorious demi-star brass lantern casts interesting prisms of light which bounce off all four walls in a room.

Pendant Lights

Pendants are the most common domestic light fittings. Usually they hang by a flex or a metal stem from the centre of a ceiling. They can range from simple rise-and-fall pendants to grand, ornate, gilded chandeliers.

Single pendants provide general background light and offer more flexibility if fitted with a dimmer switch. A careful choice of shade can also alter the quality of light cast. If using a large, open lampshade, fit a crown-silvered bulb to diffuse the light a little. Be careful to take height into consideration when fitting an overhead pendant. You don't want tall family members or guests bumping into big, low-hung fittings.

Downlighters and wall-washers

Recessed halogen downlighters and wall-washers can be fixed into ceilings. They cast pleasing washes of light on to a room to highlight specific features, bathing walls in a stream of accent lighting.

Ceiling light

Recessed downlighter

Pendant light

Wall light

Standard lamp

Wall-washer

Spotlights on tracking

Floor and Wall uplighters

Table lamp

Desk lamp

Recessed strip light

Above Light fittings are incredibly varied, and their use must always be borne in mind when choosing the ones you need.

Wall lights Wall-mounted fittings which direct and diffuse light in a variety of ways depending on the material of the housing. Useful for background, accent and information lighting, they include conical spheres, traditional wall sconces, and finials complete with lampshades. They can make a room look bigger by drawing the eye to its edges.

It is a good idea to view wall lights switched on before you buy them, since these fittings are often chosen for their decorative merit rather than their lighting capacity.

If you want to create a general soft light, use a wall fitting which throws light upwards.

Above A pretty reproduction Edwardian table lamp will enhance any period interior.

Right Although uplighters often tend to be ultra-modern in their styling, they make wonderful floor lamps for accent lighting.

Uplighters Usually freestanding and portable, uplighters project light upwards. This then bounces illumination off the ceiling to provide an atmospheric background light that is a more soothing alternative to an overhead pendant. Uplighters can also be wall-mounted. They tend to be used for general and accent lighting in kitchens, living rooms, workrooms and bathrooms. Available in modern and traditional designs.

Standard floor and table lamps These lamps are able to throw light on to different planes and into a specific area to introduce colour and character into a decorative scheme. They are the most common form of domestic lighting after the central overhead pendant.

Being freestanding and portable, floor and table lamps come in various heights, either to sit on a floor or a surface. They enhance any general or accent scheme or provide a strong source of light in their own right. They are versatile for reading by or as additional portable lighting.

Tungsten-halogen table lamps are the best light source for reading since they cast a light that is very similar to daylight. Position floor and table lamps in such a

way that you cannot see into the lampshade from above if standing or from below, when sitting down.

Spotlights These adaptable, functional fittings can be mounted on the ceiling, walls and even the floor, using lengths of lighting track. They will draw attention to worktops or specific objects such as pictures or pieces of pottery. Great for accent lighting in kitchens, living rooms, workrooms and bathrooms.

Above *Adjustable spotlights are invaluable in a kitchen, where they can be angled to provide light where and when you need it.*

Strip lighting Most commonly used in kitchens, bathrooms and garages, fluorescent strip lighting is not very attractive, so is usually concealed under shelves or behind coving. But it does offer complete illumination where required. New compact versions give off a less harsh light and are long-lasting.

Desk lamps Desk lamps provide task light exactly where you want it, on a desk, along a hall table or to highlight a mantelpiece, for example. If using a low-voltage version, make sure that the reflector provides even light with no 'hot' or 'dead' spots.

Translucent lampshades tend to spread light horizontally in the same way as daylight. Open-topped shades provide uplight by reflecting beams of light off the ceiling.

LIGHT BULBS, SWITCHES AND LAMPSHADES

BULBS

Right The range of light bulbs now available is very wide. Here is a selection which illustrates the main types on the market.

Lighting technology has undergone a dramatic transformation during the last two decades, with an ever-increasing number of styles of bulbs becoming available. The two most common light sources are the traditional tungsten filament bulb (also known as the incandescent bulb), which has been in service for more than 100 years, and the fluorescent tube, its big commercial rival since the late 1930s. However, recent developments have seen the introduction of tungsten-halogen and metal halide lighting. The last type is already common for garden lighting and is gradually being developed for use in commercial and domestic lighting schemes.

Generally speaking, you can now select a bulb to suit your particular lighting demands. The classic tungsten bulb is most suitable for overhead and occasional task lighting. Small candle bulbs work well in overhead hanging lights and in wall lights. Fluorescents are both energy saving and efficient for lighting work areas and are increasingly available in low-voltage versions that cast a more flattering light. Tungsten-halogen bulbs work well in recessed ceiling lights and in modern table lamps, and there are the more specialized bulbs such as metal halide but these should be reserved for outdoor use.

Below A low-voltage light bulb that will last for up to 5000 hours.

The higher the wattage of the bulb, the brighter and whiter is the light produced. Most bulbs can be bought in a range of 40-150 watts (although powerful outdoor lights are often 500 watts), so choose the strength of bulb according to your requirements.

For an overhead or standard lamp in the living room, bedroom or bathroom, choose 60 watts or upwards. The most suitable bulb for muted background lighting in all rooms is 40 watts, while recessed halogen lights can take 50, 100, 150 or 250 watts. Spotlight bulbs are available as PAR 38 lamps, either as spotlights or as floodlights (for outdoor use). Spotlights are available as regular, crown-silvered or dichroic reflector versions. The latter two reduce glare which is particularly important for kitchens

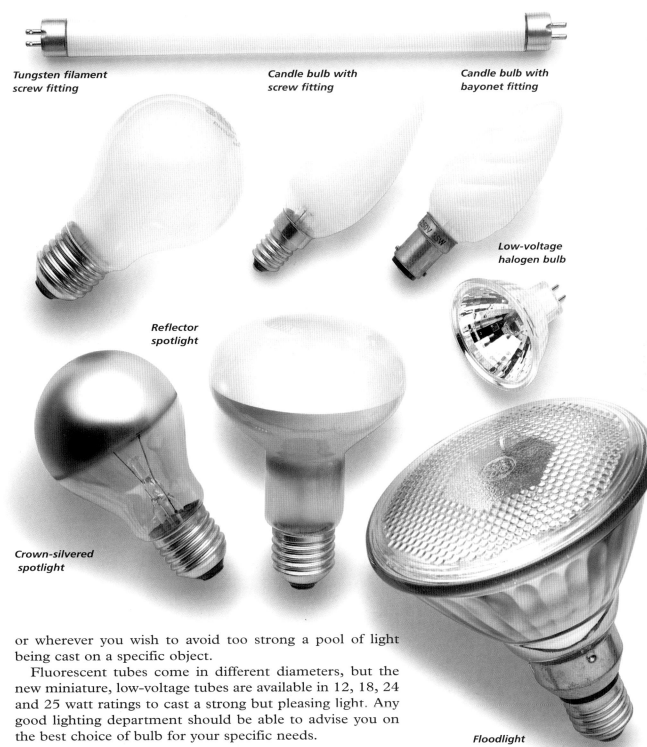

Fluorescent tube

Tungsten filament screw fitting

Candle bulb with screw fitting

Candle bulb with bayonet fitting

Low-voltage halogen bulb

Reflector spotlight

Crown-silvered spotlight

Floodlight

or wherever you wish to avoid too strong a pool of light being cast on a specific object.

Fluorescent tubes come in different diameters, but the new miniature, low-voltage tubes are available in 12, 18, 24 and 25 watt ratings to cast a strong but pleasing light. Any good lighting department should be able to advise you on the best choice of bulb for your specific needs.

WHAT'S WHAT

Tungsten filament

The most common light source, it gives a warm, yellow light which can be dimmed and is what most of us consider to be the standard light bulb.

Cheap to buy and universally used, tungsten filament bulbs come in a variety of shapes and fittings. Varieties include pearlized, clear or coloured glass, crown-silvered reflective surfaces (for spot-lighting without glare), and candle shapes. The higher the wattage of the bulb, the brighter the light.

Tungsten has a short life, however, and it is not energy-efficient; it also gives off a lot of heat and so can't be placed too close to paper, fabric or plastic shades.

Above Recessed tungsten-halogen ceiling lights are great for hallways and living rooms where they provide subtle background illumination.

Below The plain old tungsten-filament bulb can be used in all kinds of different lamps - table, pendant and wall among them.

Tungsten-halogen

These bulbs last longer than the filament bulb but are more costly. Tungsten-halogen produces a whiter light than ordinary tungsten and offers the closest possible match to natural daylight.

There are two types of halogen lighting: plug-in mains voltage, which is used predominantly for uplighters; and low-voltage, used mainly for downlights and track spots. Both can be dimmed.

Dimmable halogen uplighters are particularly useful for the home because these tall, thin fittings bounce indirect light back into the room off a ceiling or wall. Halogen bulbs are small and energy efficient, making good surfaces for spotlights. They are often used in spotlights and

Left *Fluorescent lighting, which can so often create a harsh, glaring light, here gently emphasizes a kitchen worktop.*

oped in compact versions for use in smaller fittings. These compact versions give off a warmer light than their larger counterparts, so they make good choices for kitchen and workroom lighting. But overall, the light is often unsympathetic to mood lighting in the home.

Metal halide A recently developed light source which is very cheap to run and does not distort colour. It is a popular choice for garden lighting in the form of high intensity discharge (HID) bulbs which comprise sodium, giving off an orange glow. At present, metal halide is mainly used for street lighting, where cost-effectiveness is more important than faithful colour. It is gradually making an appearance in domestic settings too.

Candlelight The most natural light of them all. Excellent for special occasions and entertaining, candles are once again being widely used to light living spaces. They provide a warm, welcoming and atmospheric light. But never leave them lit in an unattended room or if there are children about.

down- and uplighters.

One of the main advantages of halogen lighting is its power-to-size ratio. A great amount of white light can be generated from a pinhead, so light fittings can be ultra-slim, taking up very little space.

Because of its energy-efficiency, halogen is now widely used in shops - you'll recognize it by those thin, spiky rows of tiny, sparkly bulbs.

Fluorescent A cooler light than tungsten, fluorescent lighting gives a harsh, bluish light. Bulbs are efficient and very long lasting, so economical to use. They have recently been devel-

SWITCHES AND SOCKETS

You should choose light switches and sockets to suit your style of interior and personal taste. They are quite easy to swap over if you have particularly unsympathetic switches.

These days you don't have to be limited to the standard white plastic switches that are the most commonly available. Instead, try fitting brass switches. These come in a range of styles, from mock-Victorian and Regency to simple modern shapes with black switch mechanisms. Dimmer versions and multiple switches are also available. For an ultra-minimalist look, try the industrial-looking heavy-duty switches and sockets, made from grey steel with white plastic switches and sockets.

Dimmer switches act rather like neutral-coloured walls in a well-designed room. They provide a truly flexible backbone for the other lighting elements in a room and are straightforward to fit (see page 74).

LAMPSHADES

Lampshade styles vary even more than bulbs, and choosing a particular style can seem like a thankless task. However, there are certain general rules to apply.

If economy is your first priority, then nothing beats the good old standard paper shade. Recently, paper shades have been undergoing a revival, and there are many shapes, colours and textures on the market. They are an ideal way of casting a generous light in any room of the house. Cane and rattan shades are also cheap to buy and add cheer to an ordinary overhead light.

Pleated paper or fabric shades are classic designs which work well on all types of lights - wall, table and overhead. If you like your lighting to have a uniform style, then choose the same lampshade for each of your lights.

For a more sophisticated, traditional approach, there are the old-fashioned Victorian fabric shades fitted over a wire frame and trimmed with bobbles. These look best on solid brass or metal lamp stands.

Above *Switches and sockets need not only be white nowadays. This brass Georgian switch is one of many reproduction designs now available and they are worth searching out in order to complement your overall interior design.*

Left *Choose lampshades with care to blend in with your room.*

USING LIGHTING

Each room in the home calls for a different approach to lighting. It should be functional for kitchens and workrooms, atmospheric for bedrooms and dining rooms, and a combination of both for living rooms and bathrooms. Think about each room separately in relation to its main uses, then plan accordingly. This part of the book is designed to outline which kinds of lighting are most suitable for each room and is packed with dozens of ideas for creating superb lighting effects, economically and with style.

If you have a dark kitchen, for example, you can enliven it with pale colours on the walls and a careful choice of several light sources. Spotlights, recessed ceiling lights and specific pendant and task lamps create exciting pools of light in different areas of the room.

In a north-facing living room, you can conjure up the illusion of light and space by using uplighters and wall-washers which can be switched on during gloomy days to provide unnoticed accents of bright illumination.

Bathrooms which have no windows can be greatly improved by the use of recessed halogen lights in the ceiling and a couple of enclosed wall lights to create a feeling of natural daylight. Once you have grasped the general principles of good lighting, you can banish gloomy corners from your home forever.

Right *In this light, airy kitchen, two dramatic pendant lights sit happily above a central dining table. Together they create a 'leisure' island away from the room's work areas.*

ENTRANCES

First impressions count when entering a home, and good lighting can only contribute a further sense of welcome to your visitors, not only to make them feel comfortable, but also to act as a good safety and security measure. Lighting near an entrance should be either direct or reflected and must both illuminate your visitors and provide enough light for them to find the bell or door knocker without having to fumble.

At the same time, any artificial light should not pick out a visitor with a searchlight effect, but it should be bright enough so that the occupiers may, if desired, see visitors through a spyhole. Furthermore, for security purposes, it should be bright enough to discourage or illuminate intruders when you are away.

ENTRANCE FITTINGS

❖ Let the architecture of the house dictate your choice of fitting - a converted gas lamp for a Georgian house, or a glass cylinder for a contemporary house, for example, are suitable solutions.

❖ If you have a path or dark walkway flanked by greenery, consider installing some kind of concealed lighting at ground level or knee height, to light the way and act as additional security. It can be useful to have your house number or name lit up at night too.

❖ If you have an exposed entrance and your light fittings are to be open to the elements, be sure they are weatherproof.

❖ Avoid laterally placed fittings, as these tend to cast dark shadows across a front door.

BRIGHT IDEAS

❖ Match porch lights and outdoor wall lights to the architectural style of your house.

❖ Allow enough light so that you can see who is at your door through a window or peephole.

❖ Light long pathways with angled spots.

❖ Make sure your entrance lights don't cast dark shadows which would make a good hiding place for intruders.

❖ Fit a doorbell with an integral light or make sure your door knocker is well-lit too.

Right No one could fail to notice this grand porch attached to the side door of an old stone farmhouse. A warm, bright and inviting addition to an otherwise dark entranceway.

HALLS AND STAIRS

Despite the transitory nature of halls and passageways, they are the first thing a visitor sees in your home, so they should provide a welcoming light as well as specific light in which to deal with coats, hats and other belongings.

Halls also lend themselves to becoming a gallery space in which to hang pictures, family photographs or other artifacts. So consider installing some accent lighting in the form of decorative uplighters, to pinpoint these personal treasures.

Pools of directional light from recessed ceiling lights or tracks of spotlights can subconsciously draw you through the hall into the rest of the house. But avoid an excessive contrast between the lighting outdoors and that inside by carefully fixing the overall light level. A dimmer switch will give you greater flexibility.

The hall is not a place for freestanding lights. Trailing flexes here can be somewhat hazardous to your poor unsuspecting visitors.

Sometimes staircases are an attractive architectural feature in their own right, so make the most of them by hanging pictures and mirrors and providing dramatic, but safe, light fittings.

On a tall staircase, long pendant lights are both bright and effective but avoid a centrally-hung pendant (see below). In a cottage, blend in wall-mounted candle sconces with artificial lighting for a period feel. Or try diffuse lighting from a bowl-shaped wall fitting in a modern home: it softens shadows and adds tonal variety.

NARROW HALLS AND STAIRWAYS

❖ You can make a small, dark hallway appear brighter and more spacious by painting the walls a pale colour and then installing uplighting wall lights on both sides of the hall and stairway at regular intervals. These will widen your field of vision and emphasize the height of the ceiling.

❖ If there are cornices or mouldings at ceiling height, you can conceal fluorescent strips behind them. These will further emphasize the features and so attract the eye.

❖ Avoid a central pendant fitting as this will centralize the focus and lead to dark corners. This increases rather than detracts from the sense of narrowness.

STAIRS AND SAFETY

Safety is the major consideration when lighting stairs.

❖ Wall lights should be placed to follow the treads.

❖ You should light the bottom and top of the stairs, as well as any intermediate landing, with downward-directed light.

❖ When planning lighting for stairways, make sure that there is no strong directional light, as this will cause a glare which could be dangerous.

Left Two traditional wall lights cast a pleasing light over this delightful period landing.

LIVING ROOMS

Flexibility is the key to successful living room lighting. As so many different activities take place in the living room – from watching the television to reading and entertaining – the quantity and quality of light should be correspondingly generous and varied.

General lighting should be combined with task and accent to allow for this varied approach. Obviously the style of your home and your choice of decor and furnishings will to some extent influence your style of lighting. Of course, modern lighting can look good in a period setting, just as a couple of period pieces can enhance a pared-down, minimal interior, if used sensitively. In general, however, it is most common to match the light sources to the style of the room.

CREATING MOOD

Where once candles and a real fire gave a living room an atmospheric glow, it is not always so easy these days to incorporate real fire and flames into a room. Instead, try table lamps, floor lights or task lights dotted around the room to create a similar effect. They will break up the monotony and build interesting corners of illumination in which to display objects or emphasize individual pictures or pieces of furniture. The shadows created by such lights will also serve to rest the eye, helping everyone to relax.

Mood in a living room is also affected by the choice of furnishings, of course, but lighting can help to draw the eye towards the places you wish to make a feature of. Table lamps placed in front of richly decorated curtains will make sure that no one misses them.

OPENING OUT A SMALL, LOW-CEILINGED LIVING ROOM

Many living rooms have lowish ceilings and a nondescript square shape, lacking any architectural highlights. Here are a few ideas on how to use lighting to disguise a lack of features:

❖ Add dimmers to the fittings to vary the atmosphere.

❖ Use table lamps as supplementary lighting to create further intimacy.

❖ To increase the sense of space, position small, freestanding uplighters between individual pieces of furniture or plants and the walls. They will make the room look larger.

❖ Use freestanding or wall-mounted uplighters to reflect light on to the walls and ceiling to enhance their height.

Left This small living room boasts a dynamic and versatile lighting scheme which successfully exaggerates the width, length and height of the confined space. A restful mood is created with wall lights, table lamps and recessed ceiling lights.

ROMANCE AND ENTERTAINMENT

Never underestimate the power of candlelight to transform the mood of a room. Wall-mounted candle sconces are an inexpensive way of creating an intimate atmosphere for evening entertaining. There is something deeply comforting about flickering candlelight. It soothes, relaxes and immediately puts visitors at their ease.

However, a common misconception about watching television is that you should snuggle up on the sofa and turn all the lights out. In fact, repeated viewing in darkness will cause severe eye strain.

Instead, place a table lamp or floor light to the side of the television. If you have a small television sitting on a shelf, try installing concealed tungsten strip lighting behind it. Alternatively, position a downlight on the floor area in front of the television.

LIGHTING AREAS OF INTEREST

Spotlights, downlights or uplighters
To avoid the 'floodlit' look, create interesting individual pools of light around focal points such as fireplaces and sofas, coving and architraves, occasional tables and any object or area which you wish to emphasize. Pictures, pieces of art and large plants always benefit from being lit by spotlights, downlights or uplighters, making them stand out as decorative objects.

Opposite Identical table lamps are the perfect accompaniment to a small sofa in a tiny alcove. The lamps throw a discreet light around the space, allowing the eye to focus on the painting above the sofa.

Left Bedside table lamps are an absolute must. But they need not always be small.

Wall-mounted wall-washers
These are invaluable for creating grand sweeps of light across a wall or ceiling. A simple way of creating this effect is to install a conical uplighter on a wall. Textured bare brick walls can be greatly enhanced by sympathetic lighting.

Floor-standing uplighters
This is an easier alternative to wall-mounted wall-washers. Placing an uplighter or table lamp next to a sofa will help to make a living room feel more cosy and inviting, and leaving certain areas of the room in shadow adds to the atmosphere.

BRIGHT IDEAS

❖ Combine dimmable background and task lighting to create a well-balanced living area.

❖ Highlight any focal points such as fireplaces, favourite pictures or collections and displays with specific light sources such as wall-washers, picture lights, uplighters or wall-mounted downlighters or spotlights.

❖ Use table lamps for illuminating reading areas and task lights for intensive work for hobbies such as sewing, needlework or model-making.

❖ Divide a large, long living room by creating intimate pools of light. Use table lamps at the side of sofas to pick out seating areas.

DINING ROOMS

The dining room is one of the areas of a house where you can indulge your theatrical and romantic whims when planning lighting. A cosy dinner party can be remembered as a magical event if the dining atmosphere is subtle and remains in the background. On the other hand, insensitive lighting can ruin a splendid meal.

FOCUSING THE LIGHT

Below Lighting on a sideboard may provide enough accent light to eat by when coupled with candles on the dining table.

Right This tribute to 1960s' Scandinavian design includes two classic Danish pendant lights which have stood the test of time. Visually appealing, they also cast an excellent light for dining by.

The overhead pendant light comes into its own in the dining room, since it is important to adequately light the eating area. While you want to create an atmospheric and dramatic cast of light for dinner parties, no one person should be highlighted or dazzled by a too-bright overhead fitting. A single overhead pendant is the best choice for this job, since spotlights would inevitably throw at least one person into the limelight, bathing them with an unflattering light.

Chandeliers are an excellent choice for dining table lighting. If they are fitted with rise-and-fall pendants, so much the better, as then you can adjust the height according to how bright you want the light to be. They can be moved out of the way too if you want to move the table to one side to allow for a children's play area during the day, or to allow for cleaning chores to take place.

The smartest kind of chandelier is one which, for the utmost in versatility, takes either real candles or electric candle bulbs. A dimmer switch will enable you to further alter the light level to suit the time of day or activity, since family meals and playtime will obviously call for a brighter light level than will romantic dinner parties.

SUPPLEMENTARY LIGHTING

Wall lights If you are directing light mainly on to the dining table, lighting in the rest of the room should remain subtle, so as not to detract from the table setting. A couple of wall lights or floor-standing uplighters would enhance the overall light level without detracting from it. Make sure that they are placed a reasonable distance from the eating area though, or they will compete too much.

Candlelight While a perfect accompaniment to mood, this should not be used alone, as it does not provide enough light, and there is nothing worse than guests having to 'guess the dish' through a gloomy haze. Use it in combination with other lighting and never leave lit candles unattended.

Concealed lighting This sort of lighting fitted above the coving in an older house makes a dramatic but subtle backdrop for the main lighting source. A cheaper alternative would be to install some floor-standing directional spotlights behind plants or furniture, to create an equally atmospheric effect.

Halogen light Theatrical effects can be added for extra ambience. Try casting narrow beams of halogen light on to expanses of coloured or textured walls, to highlight the surface pattern. Make sure that any interesting pictures or objects are also subtly picked out, providing pools of individual interest to attract the attention of the diners.

Desk lamp The dining room table often doubles as an occasional work space for homework or hobbies, so keep a desk lamp on a convenient side table. It can be moved on to the table when required, or used to provide additional background lighting when dining. In addition, it can be used to light any food-serving or last-minute food preparation activities away from the dining table.

BRIGHT IDEAS

❖ Choose a single overhead pendant light with care, since it will both provide the main source of light and act as a decorative piece in its own right.

❖ Fit a dimmer switch and atmospheric wall lights or uplighters to supplement the table lighting.

❖ Consider a rise-and-fall pendant for maximum flexibility.

❖ Have an additional desk or table lamp somewhere in the room for last-minute food preparation and serving.

❖ When entertaining, make sure that the light level enhances your china and tableware.

Left A dining table placed close to a fireplace makes an intimate dining area in a small cottage. Candlelight completes the scene.

KITCHENS

The kitchen is increasingly treated as the heart of the home, the place where the whole family - and visitors - congregate naturally for a chat, to do homework, to help with the chores and to answer the phone.

As well as being a gathering place, the kitchen frequently doubles as a dining room for entertaining and, where the kitchen table is large enough, a work space and study. As such, it has become a multi-functional room where lighting should be one of the top priorities after space planning and the fitting of units and utilities.

Good lighting in a kitchen will create a welcoming and congenial atmosphere which will pay dividends by attracting company, and even help, for the cook. It also makes it a safe place in which to handle hot food and liquids, knives and other possibly hazardous items and activities. So, how do you do it?

Left A wood-panelled kitchen where everything is on display is made more intimate by two small table lamps.

Below A well-fitted kitchen in cool neutral colours has recessed ceiling fittings to throw light on to a cosy dining area.

MAKING THE MOST OF NATURAL LIGHT

Kitchen lighting must be versatile and flexible. A single pendant here will simply not be good enough. Either use a variety of different light sources, or use fittings which are multi-functional.

Make sure that any natural light is harnessed and emphasized in a kitchen. Replace any opaque glass with clear glass in doors or windows to increase the light. Where possible, extend the space outwards in the form of a lean-to conservatory and French windows, or upwards, in the form of a skylight, to enhance the availability of natural light. In dark kitchens, make sure that the walls, floor and fitted units are treated with bright, cheerful colours to keep the room jolly.

LIGHTING WORK AREAS

Once you have established the layout of your work triangle - the cooker, sink and food preparation area - and have everything in place, now is the time to make sure that all the areas are suitably well lit.

Downlighters Worktops benefit from downlighting, so that the food you are preparing is well illuminated but shadow-free. Overhead lighting would make your shadow cloud the view of the worktop and its contents.

Above This hob light doubles up as a light source for cooking by and a highlighter for a pleasing display of steel kitchen utensils.

Compact fluorescent tube strip lights These are the best form of worktop lighting and can be easily installed under wall cabinets, then disguised with a wooden lip. They are both bright and long-lasting, providing a sensible method of task lighting for food preparation areas. When you are ready to sit down and eat, the lights can be left on to act as background accent lighting.

Recessed halogen lights Alternatively, fit lights such as these or spotlights fixed above the front edge of fitted cupboards. Then you can direct the light where you need it, creating fixed pools of light. The illumination should be focused near the edge of the counter surface to ensure that neither you nor the wall cupboards will diffuse unwanted shadows on to the surface.

Ceiling spotlights Direct general light on to the cooking area by using ceiling spotlights or downlighters. Hobs and built-in ovens also benefit from a specific form of lighting to ensure safety when using them. Install a light above the cooker top or incorporate one into the cooker hood.

Above A simply styled kitchen is complemented by simple recessed ceiling lights.

LIGHTING EATING AREAS

When a kitchen is also used as a dining room, it is important to be able to tone down the lighting for evening meals.

Overhead pendants

Fix a pendant above the table to give localized light and to throw the rest of the room into dark relief. Keep a few of the other light sources, such as under-cupboard lights, cooker hood light or ceiling spot-lights, switched on so that you can see to serve the food. These individual pools of light will also help to create alternative atmospheric lighting for the evening.

Candles Supplement the pendant light (which should be dimmable) with candles for evening dining. Also, depending on the style of your decor, consider fitting candle wall sconces.

BRIGHT IDEAS

❖ Provide a mixture of ceiling fittings and task lighting to make a flexible lighting system.

❖ Where possible, provide separate lighting for the work surfaces in the form of strip lighting.

❖ Highlight and accent light is more important than general, over-head lighting in a kitchen.

❖ Mix functional and atmospheric lighting for the best effect.

BATH-ROOMS

Just as bedrooms look best with romantic and indulgent lighting, so bathrooms should combine safe, practical task lighting with a calm, subdued atmosphere in which to relax in a bubble-filled bath.

Make sure that all your individual tasks are taken into consideration when planning your bathroom lighting, especially if you like to linger in the bath with a good book or prefer to shave in the shower rather than in front of an extending mirror.

Right *Combination lighting works well in this bathroom. Wall lights illuminate the sink and a mirror above, while concealed lighting throws a flattering shadow on to the bath.*

SAFETY IN THE BATHROOM

❖ Water and electricity can be a lethal combination, so here, more than anywhere else in the house, do ensure that your chosen light fittings are safe and functional.

❖ Wall switches must be placed outside the door; only pull-on switches are legally acceptable for inside the room in Britain, while other countries also have specific regulations relating to bathrooms. To be on the safe side, check local restrictions before installing any bathroom lighting or wiring.

❖ Make sure that wet areas around baths and showers are truly watertight before having lighting installed in these areas.

❖ Check that fittings are fully waterproof where necessary and employ a professional electrician to install any complex lighting systems here. If you are feeling adventurous, you could investigate garden and outdoor light fittings for the bathroom, since these also have to be waterproof.

MIRROR LIGHTING

You see yourself at your best and at your worst in the bathroom mirror: first thing in the morning and last thing before going out for a night on the town. So lighting here is important, if only to reinforce your self esteem.

Mirror lighting should be soft, without shadows and clear but kind. The most useful fittings are the traditional theatrical make-up lights – either a row of low-wattage tungsten bulbs or long incandescent halogen tubes. These strip lamps should surround the mirror on at least two sides, and ideally on all four. A number of dim bulbs will make a less glaring strip than will fewer, brighter bulbs, which could easily dazzle the onlooker. Another way of achieving the same effect would be to place a wall-mounted light on either side of the mirror.

BRIGHT IDEAS

❖ Use mirrors to spread either daylight or artificial light and to enlarge what is often the smallest room in the house.

❖ For atmospheric bath times, place a few candles around the edge of the bath for a truly relaxing soak.

❖ Make the most of tungsten strip lighting by incorporating it below shelves or mirrors, to flatter skin tones and to create additional general lighting in the bathroom.

LIGHTING FOR WINDOWLESS BATHROOMS

Quite often in older houses, bathrooms have been specially created by isolating part of an original, larger room. These spaces can easily make dingy, unappealing places for your daily ablutions if not lit properly.

Directional down-lighters Use these to enhance the space, focusing them on to the walls.

Mirror lights Make sure that your mirror is quite large and lit vertically on each side. If possible, wire the mirror lights to the same switch as the overhead halogen downlights. In that way you will have an instant - but discreet - light every time you enter the bath-room, no matter what time of the day it is.

Overhead halogen lights As light will be needed during the day and at night, halogen lighting is a way of making up for the lack of daylight. Try fitting bathroom-approved, low-voltage downlighters to provide a subtle background light. These lights are prefer-able as they will not produce an ageing, unflattering light.

Left *A well-lit mirror means you will always see yourself in your best light.*

Above *Grand lighting for a grand bathroom in the form of globe-shaped wall lights.*

BEDROOMS

Bedrooms should be both romantic and functional. Many bedrooms have to double up as workrooms or quiet reading areas when space is limited, so plan your lighting according to its functions.

As this room is least used during the day, you can indulge your creative lighting whims here without fearing ridicule from friends or family. Experiment with fantasy wall lights or sentimental decorative wall sconces. Let romance carry you away and create a softly-lit draped bed, or use wall-washers to emphasize a specific paint treatment, architectural feature or piece of art.

The only practical considerations which should hinder your flights of imagination are task or table lamps on either side of the bed for reading by, and a wall switch to allow you instant light on entering the room.

Right A romantic window seat in soft pastel shades is enhanced by a plaited lampstand and a toning shade.

Below A table lamp doubles as an accent light source for a collection of prints mounted on the wall.

LIGHTING FOR MIRRORS AND STORAGE

Dressing tables should be placed near natural light and supplementary lighting provided in front of, rather than behind, your seated figure. To avoid unflattering glare at dressing table mirrors, illuminate them from their edges rather than from overhead.

If you have a wall-mounted, full-length mirror, then direct a flexible overhead light on to it. It is best to angle it at 45 degrees to where you normally stand in order to avoid glare.

If you have large, walk-in wardrobes, consider fitting a small strip light just over the door. This is then activated when the door is opened. Alternatively, fit a simple strip light that has an integral pull switch. Each of these options helps to avoid having to grope around in the dark for your clothes and shoes.

MAKING A HIGH-CEILINGED BEDROOM MORE COSY

❖ Create a sense of intimacy by focusing all the light downwards. This will keep the ceiling in partial shadow and allow the light to be concentrated on the lower part of the room.

❖ Make sure that your bedside table lamps are fitted with tungsten-filament bulbs so as to produce a warm, yellow glow. Further emphasize this by fitting warmly coloured lampshades.

❖ If you have a central pendant fitting, extend the flex on it to lower the light and decrease the spread of uplighting throughout the room.

Above *Under these charming eaves two table lamps and an overhead lantern are all that are required for a calm and cosy atmosphere.*

Right *For keeping warm in winter, use lots of candles. This inventive pelmet is made from a gnarled tree branch draped with fairy lights to add sparkle to a cold evening.*

BRIGHT IDEAS

❖ For bedside reading, nothing beats the conventional table lamp. An adjustable lamp can be angled to provide reading light or to emphasize a picture or wall, depending on its position. Otherwise, try wall-mounted spotlights or incorporate light fittings in to your bed head.

❖ Remember that if you plan to reorganize the room at any stage, then you are safer to stick with freestanding table lamps.

❖ An even more flexible and space-saving option is a clip-on spotlight attached to the bed head.

❖ For the ultimate in drama lighting, try placing a floor-standing uplighter at each corner of the bed.

❖ Since your eyes will inevitably be drawn towards the ceiling once you are in bed, avoid elaborate central overhead lighting. This will leave the corners of the room in darkness and create too much of a feature above your head.

CHILDREN'S ROOMS

The most important lighting requirement for a child's nursery or bedroom is a dimmer switch for the overhead light. From birth onwards it is an invaluable aid to both parents and children. When planning lighting for a child's room, make sure that there are enough wall sockets too, since children do not stay small for very long and they will eventually need additional task lighting for homework, computers and music systems.

LIGHTS FOR EVERY NEED

Low-level lights These can be left on throughout the night for tiny babies, so that peaceful night-time sleep will not be curtailed by a tired parent tripping over in the gloom.

Wall, table and ceiling-mounted lights Generally speaking, stick to these for the early years. Freestanding standard lamps or uplighters should be confined to the living room if there are young children in the house, since these present unnecessary hazards for the mobile baby or toddler.

Glowing plugs These plugs produce a very muted light and are particularly useful for young children who prefer to have a light on when going to sleep, or who may have their sleep disturbed by nightmares. Waking up to a gentle light may be enough to soothe their troubled sleep – and allow their parents to continue their slumber too.

Novelty table lights Another way of providing a continuous but gentle light throughout the night is by means of a small novelty table light fitted with a very low-wattage bulb. Suitable for the older child who may want to switch on a light during the night, the range of styles includes everything from china toadstools to cartoon characters.

Several manufacturers now produce table lamps which consist of a coloured glass bowl, upturned on a stand, which projects different-coloured shapes on to the ceiling, at the same time as playing a lullaby. These have proved popular, partic-

Above *Ring the changes in a growing child's room by regularly updating fabric lampshades to suit your child's age and personality.*

ularly as they play for a few minutes and then turn themselves off – hopefully when your child has dropped off to sleep.

BRIGHT IDEAS

❖ Use dimmer switches for overhead lights in the nursery.

❖ Provide some form of night light for nocturnal wakings.

❖ For older toddlers and children, provide a novelty table light.

❖ Make sure there are enough wall sockets for the growing child to have enough task lighting for school work and reading.

WORKROOMS

In many homes, a work space may well form part of another room, such as a living room, dining room, kitchen or spare bedroom. If this is the case, its lighting demands will have to be tempered accordingly. The most suitable solution would be a good, classic task light such as an Anglepoise, a French industrial lamp or, for a clearer, whiter light, a halogen desk lamp, to provide strong directional light for writing, reading or computer work.

If you are fortunate enough to have a whole room to use as a study, office or workshop, combine task lighting with general background lighting to suit your needs. If you have a workshop incorporating a workbench, make sure that the whole of the work area is well illuminated, particularly if you are likely to use potentially dangerous electrical equipment or perform repairs.

STUDY LIGHTING

Right *This classic study light with its green glass shade is both functional and attractive.*

Task lights In a study, lighting should be designed to focus on the page or computer or typewriter keyboard, rather than throwing shadows or glare on to the screen. In the case of a computer, which calls for good general lighting, make sure that it is of a similar intensity to that of the display screen to avoid glare.

Downlighters

Bookshelves and other areas of storage also benefit from specific lighting. Place angled down-lighters to shine just in front of the shelves, so that the books are visible and no shadows are thrown across them. Or place an angled clip-on spotlight on the edge of bookcase.

Background lights

When working in the small hours, it is wrong to think that light from a single desk lamp is atmospheric for the hard working, creative thinker. This type of lighting at night will cause severe eye strain if there is no other light source switched on. Make sure that there is additional light in the form of a standard lamp elsewhere in the room to reduce the contrast level between the work space and its surroundings.

BRIGHT IDEAS

❖ Combine task lighting with background lighting to avoid eye strain.

❖ Ensure that specific work areas are not in any shadow.

❖ Plan to have plenty of sockets in a workshop or area containing a workbench for all those power tools.

❖ Light bookshelves with downlighters so that everything is visible and easy to locate.

CONSERVATORIES

As conservatories consist mainly of glass panels they have their own, very specific, lighting requirements. At night, the glass becomes a reflector so any light source should be shielded to avoid glare. It is best to use directional light, either angled down from the roof or in the form of numerous low-level lamps, preferably low-voltage. These have the double advantage of providing low-glare, specific washes of light, and enable you to focus attention on special plants or pieces of furniture.

Coloured bulbs and natural candlelight work especially well in conservatories, where the reflected light provided by the glass walls creates atmospheric shadows and colours which bounce around the room in a romantic and enchanting manner.

Since a lot of conservatory furniture is made from cane and rattan, low-level light placed behind or around these pieces will also create fascinating shadows to further complete a magical atmosphere. Here is the place to relax, read or entertain under the stars.

DINING LIGHTING

Many conservatories double up as dining rooms or as places for entertaining so do consider lighting them accordingly.

Conical wall-washers Where there are exposed brick walls, conical wall-washers will throw sheets of light across the bricks. This emphasizes them and creates interesting textures.

Pendant lights An ideal choice is a metal chandelier housing either candle bulbs or real candles. It weighs little, is not too solid and can be easily fixed to an overhead roof beam.

Right A verdigris five-arm pendant light fitted with electric candle bulbs is a perfect solution for a dining room or conservatory. It is both stylish and practical, especially if fitted with a dimmer switch.

Above Candlelight which reflects off the glass walls of a conservatory adds sparkle to any night-time entertaining.

Candles Don't forget the magic of candles for the dining table. A subtly lit conservatory is one of the great joys of successful home lighting, providing a special place away from the bustle of the rest of the house.

BRIGHT IDEAS

❖ Use coloured bulbs in low-level spotlights to create dramatic pools of light.

❖ Echo the natural flickerings of the night sky by using candles in wall sconces, overhead candelabra or in candlesticks on the table.

❖ Throw spotlights on to specific pieces of furniture or behind plants to make interesting areas of brightness.

❖ Use dimmer switches for any overhead lights in order to vary the light source.

❖ Provide table lamps for seating areas so you can read in peace and comfort.

GARDENS

There is something quite magical about a well-lit garden. Greenery provides an atmospheric backdrop for evening entertaining or relaxing if well spotlighted. Subtle lighting outdoors will also enhance your indoor space, making the room which backs on to the garden seem as if it has an outdoor extension. Electric lights combined with natural light sources such as outdoor flares and candles will make you wish you could sleep under the stars.

When thinking about outdoor lighting, bear in mind your locality. If you back on to a street or have neighbours close by on each side of you, they may not be too keen on nightly illuminations for company. For this reason, keep light levels fairly low in a garden - unless, of course, you live in a secluded house in the middle of the countryside.

Left *A beautifully lit garden makes an inviting evening retreat. Powerful lights have been carefully placed to shine onto each flower bed, emphasizing the colourful plants.*

GARDEN LIGHTING

Low-angle lights The best way to cast light in a garden is to install many low-angle lights at or near ground level. A combination of several pools of light and the corresponding dark shadows which they create will make a marvellous sight when viewed from indoors.

All specialist garden lights are made from high-grade materials which are waterproof and resist corrosion. Many outdoor lights are now designed to take the new energy efficient compact fluorescent bulbs. But remember that these are not dimmable, so choose a low-wattage unit. Check local regulations for further constraints on which types of fitting are most suitable.

Flares If you do not have the financial resources available for the additional expense of running waterproof electric cables under the ground and into your garden, then flares are the answer. Although temporary, they have the added advantage of being used only when you need them.

Right The transition from indoors to outdoors is here delightfully blurred with greenery and sparkling lights - ceiling and wall fittings pinpoint specific areas of foliage, bringing the outside in.

Garden flares present an inexpensive and versatile way of creating portable lights outdoors. They are available in many different heights and colours and will add atmosphere to any barbecue or party. For the best effect, place them in front of walls, among plants (but away from any dense patches of greenery which could be a fire hazard). The flickering flames will produce endless interesting shadows around the garden.

Candles Like flares, candles in the garden on a still night create the most marvellous atmosphere. Substantial outdoor scented candles in containers such as terracotta pots and galvanized metal buckets are becoming increasingly popular. These are both decorative and functional.

Fairy lights By installing an exterior socket (or by utilizing an extension flex from a garage, shed or even the kitchen), you can also use outdoor fairy lights for an instant party atmosphere. Trailed through a modest-sized tree or large shrub, they will provide a sparkling, celebratory glow over your guests. Try white bulbs for subtlety, coloured ones for fun and frivolity.

BRIGHT IDEAS

❖ If your garden consists of specific areas of interest or activity, such as a patio, pond, pergola or arbour, or a lovely wall of climbers, then make the most of these features by highlighting them at night.

❖ Paths should have punctuated light along them to lead people along, while trees can be spotlit from below, or festooned with decorative bulbs. If a tree is placed against a wall, wash it with light so that the silhouette of the tree is highlighted.

❖ Water is an especially evocative medium for creating sparkling light. In a pond, consider installing a submersible fountain unit which produces a broad jet of water and light it with a precise beam of light. The brightly lit dancing drops will delight both you and your guests.

Security lights If you are lighting the outside of your house for security and safety reasons (see pages 68-9), you might like to think about specific features which merit special lighting. Architectural details such as interesting eaves, doors, windows or roofs, for instance, can be best lit by angled lights at ground level.

SECURITY

Security lighting has become more sophisticated in recent years and there are now several ways of lighting the way to your door. You can either use lighting attached to the side of your home or lighting installed in the garden.

Wall lighting is the easiest to install, as you can control the lights from indoors and link them to the mains via cables passing through brickwork or along window sills. Garden lighting, however, is more complicated since it can be mains- or low-voltage – a qualified electrician should always be consulted for outdoor lighting work. When placing lights, make sure you don't create pockets of shadow which can end up giving shelter to burglars.

Above *Fitting security lights at the entrance to your house is both sensible and practical.*

SECURITY SYSTEMS

Floodlights While the most common forms of outdoor lighting are porch lights, bulkheads or illuminated signs, the best form of deterrent is a mains-voltage,

Below *Security lighting can also double up as garden lighting – floodlights work very well in this way.*

500-watt halogen floodlight. House-mounted floodlights can be linked up to an electronic timer so that they needn't be on all night. Even more sophisticated are those that include a passive infrared sensor which activates the light on detection of body heat. You can buy a sensor either integrated into a light fitting or independent of it.

Alarm systems In addition, there are now electronic alarm systems which are activated if doors or windows are tampered with. An alarm signal indoors sets off bright lighting and an audible alarm. Although more expensive to install, these systems mean that you

do not have to keep lights on constantly. Also, the fact that a burglar would need to use a torch to see how to force entry through doors and windows, would bring attention to them if seen by neighbours.

Several manufacturers have now come up with total packages to build infra-red security into garden lighting. Although tricky to install, it is flexible, so you can use it at strategic points around the house.

Independent sensors Although more complicated, a sensor such as this has an advantage over built-in designs, because you can place it wherever you want to catch intruders unawares.

BRIGHT IDEAS

❖ Don't let security override comfort - there's nothing worse than enjoying the sunset on your patio when two insensitive 500-watt floodlights come on right in your face.

❖ Don't swamp your neighbours' gardens with light from your floodlighting system.

❖ Keep all controls for your outdoor security lighting indoors.

❖ Don't let the placing of infra-red sensors or trailing cables interfere with chores such as hedge cutting or lawn mowing.

❖ There is a snag with infra-red systems - the sensor is all too easily triggered by cats or dogs, who could play havoc with your security lighting.

❖ When programming your indoor lights to go on and off at odd times, it is more cost effective to replace conventional tungsten halogen bulbs with fluorescent ones. Their long life means that they cost less to operate.

BASICS

Once you have chosen your lighting requirements, the next task is to think about how you are going to get them installed. By far the safest proposition is to employ a fully qualified electrician to carry out any major jobs such as rewiring or installing new sockets. Fiddling with electricity is one of the most dangerous and possibly fatal tasks which the home DIY-er can undertake, so do not attempt any task which you are not one hundred per cent sure about.

Contact several electricians for quotations before making a final decision, and try to save up several jobs at a time to make the project more cost effective. If you are thinking of installing an outdoor light, for instance, wait until you have some repairs or extra interior socket requirements before calling in a professional.

There are strict guidelines which vary from country to country about how and where you should wire up domestic electricity supplies. Without this knowledge, it is just too risky to install any additional lighting or supply circuits on your own. Always consult a professional who is a member of the national register of qualified electricians (see Suppliers on page 77 for addresses). Your local utility company should also be able to provide a list of reliable electricians if you do not know of any through personal recommendation.

As well as information on safety and understanding fuse boxes, this section gives you some basic information on changing overhead pendants and fitting a dimmer switch. These are jobs which can be successfully undertaken as long as you ALWAYS remember to switch off your electricity supply before starting work.

Right *By consulting a professional electrician before embarking on any major lighting installation you can be sure of a safe and effective result.*

SAFETY

Before undertaking ANY electrical work around the home, you should consider the following safety criteria. More than any other DIY work, the fitting of electrical wiring or lighting can prove fatal.

Consider employing a professional electrician for even minor jobs around the home such as installing ceiling fittings or simple rewiring. It could save your life.

SAFETY TIPS

❖ Never undertake any task unless you have complete confidence that you can carry it out successfully and safely.

❖ When carrying out any electrical work in the home, turn off the main isolating switch before starting work. If you are working on only one circuit, remove the appropriate circuit fuse (or turn off the miniature circuit breaker) before turning the main switch back on to restore power to the rest of the house.

❖ When wiring, double-check all connections to ensure that the cores are connected to the right terminals. Check also that they are securely fitted and that no bare conductor is visible.

❖ If working on plug-in lights, disconnect them from the socket before starting your task.

❖ An earth conductor is always essential. Any fitting with metal parts should have an earth terminal on it, and should be wired up with three-core flex.

❖ Avoid trailing flexes and overloaded adaptors. Always install more outlets if they are required.

CIRCUIT FAILURE

❖ A failure in several lights or fittings at once means that one of the circuit fuses has blown in the mains fuse box. The cause may be a faulty socket, plug or appliance, an overloading of the circuit, or a fault in the actual wiring of the circuit.

❖ To rewire a blown fuse: remove the old wire and any blobs of metal, loop the new wire clockwise round the screw at one end, pass it through the holder and loop it clockwise round the screw at the other end. You will need 5-amp fuse wire for lighting and 30-amp wire for power circuits.

❖ If a circuit-breaker fuse has 'tripped' (switched off), just switch it on again, once you have sorted out the problem.

❖ In the case of a cartridge-type mains circuit fuse, simply replace it with a new fuse.

UNDERSTANDING FUSE BOXES

All electricity enters a house via an over-head or underground cable, which runs into the electricity company's main service fuse. This allows you to draw a certain amount of power from the system.

The cable then runs on to your electricity meter and to your fuse box or consumer unit. All the equipment up to and including the meter is the property of the utility company and should not be interfered with at any time.

A modern fuse box usually consists of a unit containing the main on-off switch for the house's overall electricity supply. In addition, there are a number of circuit breakers (MCBs), each labelled and/or colour coded to show which type of circuit it covers. The usual format is 5amp (white) for lighting, 30amp (red) for power circuits, as well as 15amp (yellow) and 20amp (blue) for special circuits to individual appliances. Inside the unit there is often a chart identifying each circuit. If this information is missing, compile a list as and when you discover which circuit is which (ie kitchen main circuit, upstairs lighting, etc.). It will be useful for you and for any electrician called in to carry out work for you.

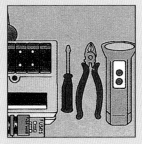

Keep a torch near the fuse box together with wire cutters, a screwdriver, spare fuse wires and cartridge fuses for plugs.

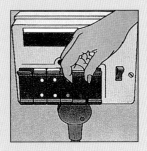

A failure in several lights or fittings at once means that one of the circuit fuses has blown in the mains fuse box. The cause may be a faulty socket, plug or appliance, an overloading of the circuit, or a fault in the actual wiring of the circuit.

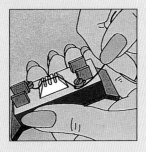

To rewire a blown fuse: remove the old wire and any blobs of metal, loop the new wire clockwise round the screw at one end, pass it through the holder and loop it clockwise round the screw at the other end.

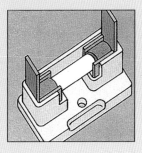

If a circuit-breaker fuse has 'tripped' (switched off), just switch it on again, once you have sorted out the problem. In the case of a cartridge-type mains circuit fuse, simply replace with a new fuse.

WIRING A PLUG

Only use plugs marked BS1363 as they conform to British Standards and so are safe. All square-pin plugs have a small cartridge fuse to protect the appliance - 3amp (red) for appliances of up to 720W or 13amp (brown) for those from 720 to 3000W.

HOW TO WIRE A 13 AMP PLUG

1 Remove the cover by loosening the large screw between the pins and then lever out the fuse. Position the flex on the open plug to see how much of the outer sheathing you will need to remove. Remember that the cord clamp must grip the sheath, not the wires within.

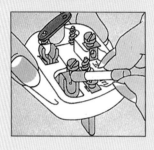

2 Strip the sheathing and then cut the conductors to the right length by holding the flex against the plug once again. Check that the wires take the most direct routes to their terminals and lie neatly in the plug's channels.

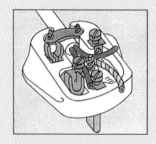

3 Strip and prepare the ends of the wires in the same way and then secure each to its terminal. If you are using two-core flex, wire to the live and neutral terminals only, leaving the earth terminal empty.

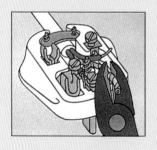

4 Tighten the cord clamp to grip the end of the sheathing and secure the flex. Put a fuse of the correct rating in place and then replace the cover and tighten the screw.

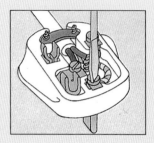

FITTING A DIMMER SWITCH

Before buying a new dimmer switch, examine the present switch to see what type of wiring feeds it and then buy a dimmer to accommodate it.

WHAT TO DO

1 Dimmer switches are serviced by a two-core and earth cable, and the earth conductor (if there is one) is connected to an earth terminal on the mounting box. Connect the red and black wires to the terminals - they can be connected either way round.

2 Check on the inside of the faceplate which is the top - it will be marked top - and screw in place. It is important to get the faceplate on the right way or the off position of the dimmer switch will be on the wrong side which could be confusing.

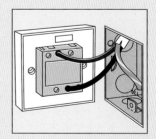

REPLACING A CEILING PENDANT

Any lighting work should be begun in the morning so that you don't run out of daylight, and ladders must reach halfway up your body while also being in easy reach of the job. Never stand on chairs to reach overhead light fittings.

IMPORTANT: Do not rely on simply turning off the light switch, as the circuit cables at the ceiling rose will still be live. Isolate the circuit you need to work on by removing the corresponding circuit fuse at the fuse box. Put it in your pocket where no one can get at it.

WHAT TO DO

Most pendant lamps will hang from or fit over the type of rose described here via some kind of special fitting which is usually supplied. The exception is a globe light with a flat plate that screws to the ceiling, in which case you'll have to fit the rose into the ceiling space.

If you only have two wires to deal with, the circuit is not earthed and if your new fitting is made of metal it is essential that you provide an earth back to the earth terminal in your fuse box. For this you will need 1.5mm single-core green/yellow insulated cable. Ideally, though, you should consider having your whole system rewired as it will be outdated and dangerous in this state.

1 Take off the lampshade, if there is one. To replace an existing pendant light you will probably need to remove the ceiling rose (baseplate) and its flex, so unscrew the ceiling rose cover. If the ceiling has been redecorated many times, you will need to loosen the cover by running a handyman's knife around the edge.

2 Slide the baseplate down the flex. Hold the flex with one hand and use a small screwdriver in the other one to disconnect the circuit cable from the terminal block.

3 Then disconnect the wires coming from the old light and rewire the new ceiling pendant.

4 Screw the baseplate to the conduit already attached to the ceiling. If you have a really heavy fitting, you might find it necessary to fix the conduit and baseplate to the floor above forming a fixing between the joists.

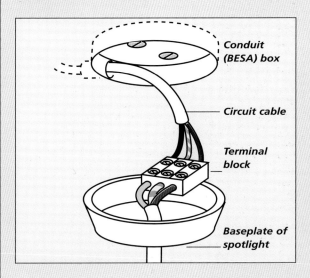

Conduit (BESA) box

Circuit cable

Terminal block

Baseplate of spotlight

BRIEFING AN ELECTRICIAN

If you have moved house and require a few additional power sockets or have new ceiling fittings which need installing, try to build up several tasks at a time to make it cost effective for a qualified electrician to come and carry out all your jobs at once. It will give you peace of mind and might not be as expensive as you think.

Ensure that any electrician you employ is a member of the appropriate regulatory body. In Britain, all reliable electricians should be members of the Institution of Electrical Engineers. This means that they will be able to guarantee the safety standards of any work carried out.

BRIEFING · A CHECKLIST

❖ Carefully plan what you need lit and how you would prefer to do it. Particularly note how many sockets you may need and where they should ideally be positioned (always remember the convenience factor).

❖ Wall-washers and uplighters which need wiring channelled into the walls need particularly careful planning as once they are in place they can't be moved without huge upheavals.

❖ Consult all members of the family about their requirements too. Teenagers will probably have strong views about lighting their own 'dens', while work spaces and kitchens also merit careful consideration if you are planning to redesign these areas of a house over a period of time.

❖ Write down all your requirements so you can discuss them fully with the professionals.

❖ If you need to undertake major rewiring work or would like new lighting systems installed, you should call in at least three electricians to prepare a quotation.

STOCKISTS AND SUPPLIERS

Institution of Electrical Engineers
Savoy Place
London WC2R 0BL
0171 240 1871

The Lighting Industry Federation
Swan House
207 Balham High Road
London SW17 7BQ
0181 675 5432

National Inspection Council for Electrical Installation Contracting (NICEIC)
Vintage House
37 Albert Embankment
London SE1 7UJ
0171 582 7746

The NICEIC investigates complaints about faulty electrical installations.

Artemide
17-19 Neal Street
London WC2H 9PU
0171 836 6753

For ultra modern European lights.

Philips Lighting
Lighting division
PO Box 298
City House, London Road
Croydon CR9 3QR
0181 665 6655

Thorn Lighting Ltd
Graveland Rd
Tipton
West Midlands
DY4 7XB
0121 557 2828

John Cullen Lighting
216 Fulham Palace Road
London W6 9NT
0171 381 8944

Specialists in low-voltage lighting with a demonstration studio; telephone for an appointment.

Ikea Ltd
255 North Circular Road
London NW10 0JQ
0181 451 5944

Christopher Wray's Lighting Emporium
600 Kings Road
London SW6 2DX
0171 736 8434

Huge selection of traditional and reproduction lights with branches in large cities around the country; telephone for details of shops near you.

The London Lighting Company
135 Fulham Road
London SW3 6RT
0171 589 3612

Modern lighting.

The Light Brigade
28 Rodney Road
Cheltenham
Gloucestershire GL50 1JJ
01242 226777

Handmade, hand painted wall lights and shades; home visiting service available.

The Conran Shop
Michelin House
81 Fulham Road
London SW3 6RD
0171 589 7401

Excellent range of lights and shades.

Stiffkey Lamp Shop
Townshend Arms
Stiffkey
Wells-next-the-Sea
Norfolk NR23 1AJ
01328 830460

Restored antique lights and fittings.

Heals
196 Tottenham Court Road
London W1P 9LD
0171 636 1666

Contemporary classics.

Habitat UK Ltd
The Heals Building
196 Tottenham Court Road
London W1P 9LD
Particularly good table and floor lights.
0171 255 2545

Telephone for details of your nearest store.

British Home Stores PLC
Marylebone House
129-137 Marylebone Road
London NW1 5QD
0171 262 3288

A good range of modern and reproduction ceiling lights, wall lights and lampshades. Telephone for details of your nearest store.

John Lewis Partnership
171 Victoria Street
London SW1E 5NN
0171 828 1000

Telephone for details of your nearest store.

Mr Light
275 Fulham Rd
London SW10 9PZ
0171 352 7525

INDEX

The page numbers in *italics* represent illustrations.

ACKNOWLEDGMENTS

The author and publisher would like to thank the following companies and people for their help with supplying photographs for this book:

Front cover: (main) Wellman; HB/Trevor Richards; Pelicans PR; HB/Roy Smith; Stiffkey Lampshop.

Back cover: Condor PR.

Page 3, HB/Roy Smith; pages 4-5, HB/Jerry Tubby; page 6, HB/Peter Anderson; pages 8-9, HB/Derek Lomas; pages 10-11, Charles Barker PR; page 12, HB/Steve Hawkins; pages 12-13, HB; page 15, HB/Ian Kalinowski; pages 16-17, John Cullen Lighting; page 18, HB/Tony Timmington; page 19, HB/Ron Kelly; pages 20-1, Wellman; page 21, Cameron PR; page 22, Stiffkey Lampshop; page 24, Stiffkey Lampshop; page 25, HB/Dennis Stone; pages 26-7, Jon Stewart; page 28 top, HB/Trevor Richards; page 28 bottom, HB/Spike Powell; page 29, HB; page 30, HB/Trevor Richards; page 31, Christopher Wray; pages 32-3, HB/Tom Leighton; page 35, Pelicans PR; page 36, HB/Colin Poole; pages 38-9, Condor PR; page 40, Charles Barker PR; page 41, John Cullen Lighting; page 42, HB/Tony Timmington; page 43, EWA; pages 44-5, HB/Spike Powell; page 46, HB/Ron Kelly; page 47, HB/Roy Smith; page 48, HB/Ian Kalinowski; pages 48-9, Sheila Fitzjones PR; pages 50-1, Andrea Marks PR; pages 52-3, Halston PR; page 53, HB/Dennis Stone; page 54, Condor PR; page 55, Ken Kirkwood; page 56, HB/Trevor Richards; pages 56-7, HB/Trevor Richards; page 58, HB/Steve Hawkins; page 59, Robert Harding/Homes & Gardens; page 60, Christopher Wray; page 61, HB/Brian Harrison; page 62, Christopher Wray; pages 62-3, Pelicans PR; pages 64-5, John Cullen Lighting; pages 66-7, John Cullen Lighting; page 68 top, Christopher Wray; pages 68-9, Anthony Osmond-Evans; pages 70-1, HB/Ron Kelly.